God's Love Story:

The Story of God's Love in the Messiah's Birth
Book 9

By R. Lane Lender

STORIES OF LIFE PRODUCTIONS

God's Love Story: The Story of God's Love in the Messiah's Birth, Book 9

Copyright © 2020 By Stories of Life Productions

ISBN: 978-1-970032-16-1 (Hard Cover)

ISBN: 978-1-970032-45-1 (eBook)

For more information about Stories of Life Productions and/or God's Love Story Visual Bible visit www.glsvb.org.

All rights reserved. No part of this publication may be reproduced, stored in a retrieval system, or transmitted in any form or by any means – electronic, mechanical, photocopy, recording, or any other – except for brief quotations in printed reviews, without the prior permission of Stories of Life Productions.

Published in the United States of America

Introduction

God's Love Story Children's Book Series is dedicated to my grandchildren. One of the greatest gifts a parent can pass off to their children is a passion to love Jesus more than anything else in this world. This passion is more caught than taught. Our children need to see our love for Jesus and they too will follow in our footsteps. My wife and I are truly blessed to not only have godly parents but to have two wonderful children, now in their mid twenties, who have learned to love Jesus from birth. As I write, my son is a prosecuting attorney in Texas and my daughter is married to a wonderful man, a dedicated Christ follower. They now have one child and their hope is many more. My daughter is also preparing to homeschool them all like she and her brother were. My desire is to provide a biblically-based tool for parents to use to cultivate in their children a love for Jesus in their most precious and formative years. I desire nothing more than to see my future grandchildren come to know Jesus and to develop into solid Kingdom contributing Christ followers. Thus, I submit this contribution. My prayer is that this book series develops in your children a love for the gospel and a passion for Jesus.

I also want to thank you for your purchase of this book and the other books in this series (See the back cover for more details). Your purchase goes directly to support Stories of Life Productions as we continue to produce, promote, and distribute God's Love Story Visual Bible (GLSVB). GLSVB is an oral story Bible created for the cell phone that has been translated into several languages of Unreached People Groups (UPGs). These UPGs live in places that are very difficult to access with the gospel. Because of your purchase, as well as gifts from generous donors, GLSVB is provided free to missionaries and believers around the world who are using this tool for evangelism and discipleship. GLSVB can be accessed at www.hikayaat.com. To find out more information, order books, or help us promote God's Love Story Children's Book series or GLSVB, visit www.glsvb.org. May God's Love Story Children's Books give you and your child a passion to serve Christ and His Kingdom's purpose!

Sincerely,
R. Lane Lender
Stories of Life Productions
contact@glsvb.org
www.hikayaat.com
www.glsvb.org

The scripture gives us a wonderful story,
The Messiah came down to earth;
Mary and Joseph, the baby Jesus,
A night of Divine birth;

The story tells us of Mary's engagement,
To Joseph, a godly man;
Mary a virgin betrothed to Joseph,
A miracle child was God's plan;

One day Gabriel came to Mary saying,
"Greetings most favored one!;
Peace be to you, the Lord is with you,
You'll conceive and give birth to a Son";

"You'll call His name Jesus, He will be great,
On King David's throne He will sit;
Forever and ever, His love will reign,
He'll save all who believe from the pit";

Mary asked, "How, can all of this be,
For I am a girl innocent?";
Gabriel replied, "Our God is strong,
There's no plan He can't implement!";

Mary said, "Yes! I am your servant,"
The Lord was very pleased;
She was obedient, trusting in God,
His purpose and plan she seized;

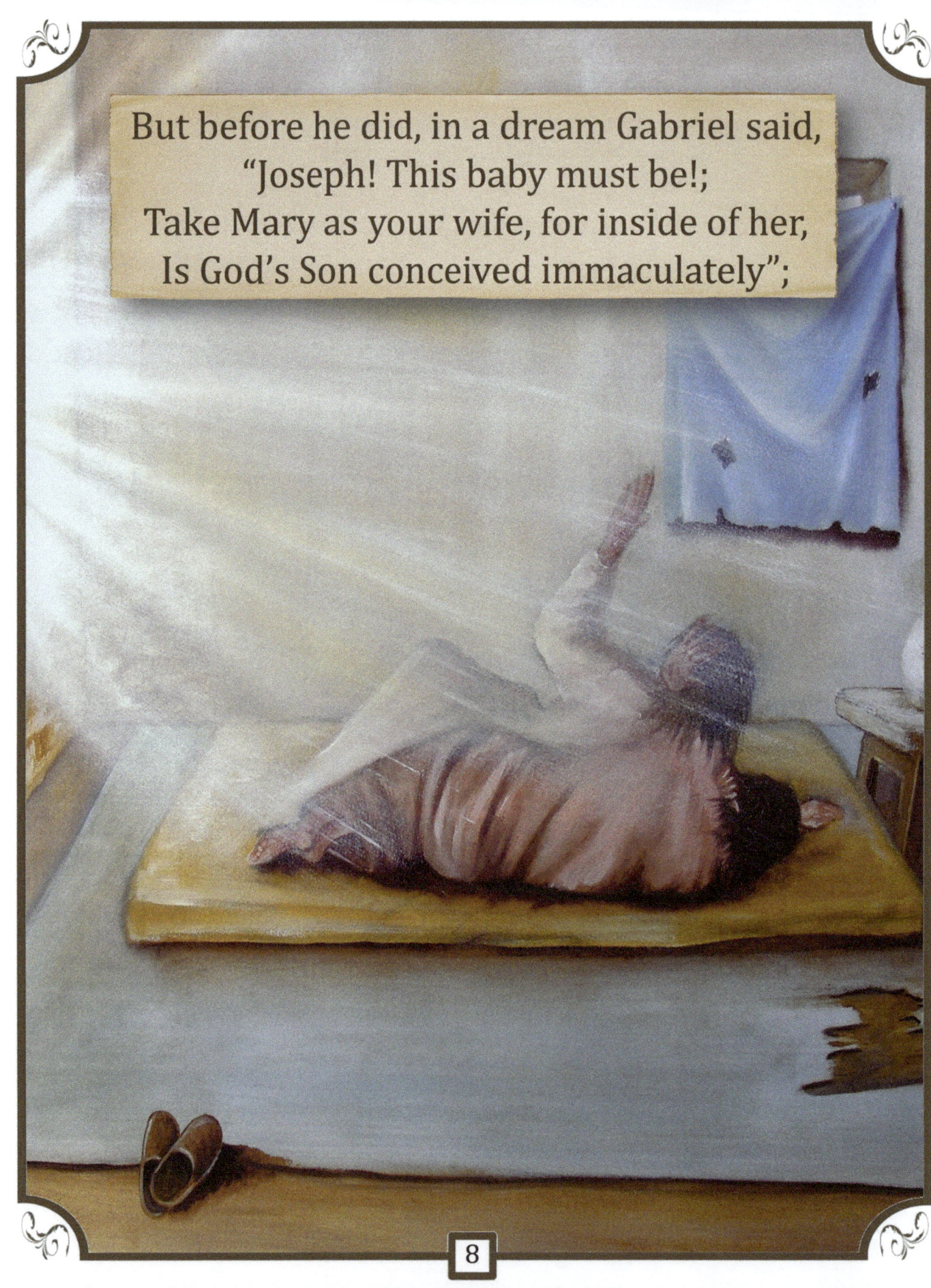

But before he did, in a dream Gabriel said,
"Joseph! This baby must be!;
Take Mary as your wife, for inside of her,
Is God's Son conceived immaculately";

Taking his wife and packing his donkey,
They left for Bethlehem's way;
From the line of David, returning to home,
Cause Joseph had taxes to pay;

When they arrived, there was no room,
For them to sleep in the Inn;
But they were able to find room in a stable,
Finding shelter and animals within;

The time had arrived, and Jesus was born,
Lowly and in a manger;
Wrapped in swaddling clothes, 10 fingers and toes,
Mary kept him from danger;

Fearing at first what this could be,
They quickly said, "Let's go see!";
They found Jesus there, a baby so lovely,
They spread the good news with glee;

Some time later, when Jesus a lad,
A star the wise men followed;
Arriving in Jerusalem and asking around,
For the King of the Jews so hallowed;

King Herod heard that they were around,
Oh so jealous was he;
Trying to trick them, He told them to tell him,
"When you find him, I too want to see";

The star came to rest over the house,
Where Jesus and his parents were;
They gave Jesus gifts, fit for a king,
Gold, frankincense and myrrh;

Warned in a dream of Herod's plan,
They returned another way;
With continued allure, privileged for sure,
They rejoiced at seeing that day!;

An angel told Joseph to return home,
When Herod the king had died;
Fearing the worst in Bethlehem,
Off to Nazareth where they would reside;

Lightning Source UK Ltd.
Milton Keynes UK
UKHW050838110920
369558UK00004B/102